Anxiety

Understanding Anxiety And Effective Strategies To Alleviate Anxiety And Fear In Pursuit Of Personal Mastery

(Efficient Approaches To Lowering Anxiety Levels, Mitigating Conflict, And Enhancing Communication Within Your Relationship)

Philippe Goodwin

TABLE OF CONTENT

Introduction 1

Effective Approaches To Alleviate Anxiety And Enhance Quality Of Life 4

Developing Authentic Self-Assurance As An Effective Measure Against Anxiety. 20

Engaging In Physical Activity For Serenity And Relaxation 25

Methodology Used In Cognitive Behavioral Therapy 43

Therapy Using Cognitive Behavior 73

Are You Feeling Stressed? The Symptoms Revealed 83

Negative Emotions 98

Frenemies Of Anxiety 104

Introduction

Enhancing your communication abilities constitutes a paramount measure for augmenting your self-assurance and overall sense of contentment. If one possesses introverted or shy tendencies to some extent, cultivating a higher degree of sociability could be the catalyst for broadening one's horizons and accessing a plethora of opportunities in life. If you belong to the category of individuals who encounter challenges in effectively engaging in interpersonal communication, struggle to convey your thoughts articulately, or experience apprehension when determining what to express, this literary work is specifically tailored to cater to your needs.

This book entails straightforward yet exceptionally valuable guidance and knowledge that will aid in the improvement of your communication abilities and social interactions. Upon completion of the reading, individuals will experience an enhanced propensity for extroversion, greater receptivity towards novel concepts, and improved verbal engagement in social interactions. This book has the potential to facilitate significant transformations in your life by providing comprehensive guidance on enhancing your social skills in various aspects of daily existence. Upon reading this book, you shall discern a notable transformation in your comportment, communication, and cognition – a change that promises undeniable positivity.

Making a conscious endeavor to effectively engage in communication with others will undoubtedly enhance various aspects of your life. Upon acquiring the skill of fostering sincere connections with others, you will undoubtedly exude an aura of assurance and competence. This, in turn, will pave the way for forging new friendships, exerting a considerable influence over others, and even attaining notable accomplishments in your professional endeavors. Through implementing alterations in your communication strategies, you will witness substantial benefits in multiple facets of your life, paving the way for eventual triumph. After familiarizing yourself with the content of this book, you will swiftly discern a notable reduction in the intensity of your apprehensions surrounding communication and social interaction. Your articulation will facilitate a more seamless expression, thereby fostering a sense of ease and comfort among the participants of a conversation. Therefore, enhance the quality of your life by engaging in the transformative experience of reading this book. Enjoy!

Effective Approaches To Alleviate Anxiety And Enhance Quality Of Life

Within these pages, you shall be acquainted with a handful of additional techniques, which are comparatively less specific in nature compared to the ones you have hitherto encountered. At this juncture, you will acquire knowledge concerning tactics that can be deployed across a broader spectrum in order to foster the transformations in your life that you aspire to witness. You will acquire knowledge on enhancing your overall quality of life as well. These strategies should be regarded as additional components integrated into this book, offering a slight augmentation of content with the aim of helping you discover an approach that truly resonates with your needs.

Techniques for Alleviating Anxiety" "Approaches to Reduce Anxiety" "Tactics for Easing Anxiety

When one is afflicted with anxiety, it can progressively become effortless to become excessively consumed by pessimism, reaching a point where the prospect of survival or liberation from such negativity appears bleak. You become trapped in a pervasive pessimistic mindset that instills within you an apprehension that this state of mind will endure indefinitely. Nonetheless, such a statement could not be more distant from veracity. It is indeed possible to attain relief from anxiety. This particular portion will present you with an additional quartet of methods through which you may attain solace in your existence, specifically targeting the realm of anxiety. It is our hope that these strategies will prove advantageous to you in varying capacities.

Realistic Thinking
This represents an additional approach to regulate emotions and engage in rational thinking. By practicing realistic thinking, one is capable of discerning between thoughts that align with reality

and those that do not. In instances where unrealistic notions arise, they can be transformed into a more rational perspective. By engaging in this action, you are effectively establishing the ability to revise thoughts as they arise.

The initial stage of this process involves acquiring awareness of the subject matter that occupies your thoughts. This is where your mindfulness techniques are invaluable—employing these strategies enables you to discern the direction of your thoughts, thereby aiding you in uncovering various loose ends and unrealistic notions. Identify the specific thoughts among the aforementioned ones that elicit negative emotions in you, and focus your efforts on addressing those particular thoughts. For instance, if you experience a sense of profound distress due to the cancellation of your regularly scheduled date night, you are harboring an impractical belief. Please take note of your emotional response and discern the underlying thought associated with it. What is the reason for your concern regarding your inability to attend the scheduled rendezvous? Indeed, this aligns with the process of discerning negative automatic cognitions. Indeed, that is precisely the course of action you are pursuing at present—you aim to discern that pessimistic thought in order to rectify it succinctly through a brief sentence.

Your response to feeling upset about the scheduled evening might stem from a desire to prevent your partner from perceiving a decline in your affection for them, as they have frequently distanced themselves from you in the past, thus prompting you to prioritize the success of this particular occasion. Upon contemplation, one may come to acknowledge that the aforementioned notion represents a substantial exaggeration in response to a mere absence from a solitary date. In this reflection, an individual may choose to reiterate to themselves that if a relationship were to disintegrate on account of a solitary instance, then it was inherently lacking in value from its inception. By rectifying that notion and imbuing it with a more optimistic perspective, you effectively resolve the issue within your cognitive faculties. You possess the capability to mitigate your emotional state as a result of encountering the veracity.

Pursuing the services of a mental health professional

Occasionally, the most effective course of action in addressing persevering anxiety entails procuring the services of a mental health professional. Although it may be tempting to believe otherwise, implementing this task is significantly more challenging than expressing it. Nevertheless, even if you are under the impression that you are exempt from requiring one, it would be prudent to contemplate its potential benefits. Therapists are not malevolent or a frivolous expense—they are in fact highly beneficial. They can assist you in navigating various types of negative thoughts and facilitate your ability to effectively manage yourself regardless of the current circumstances. By means of these procedures, you will obtain tailored content that surpasses the capabilities of a printed book. You will receive instantaneous feedback, providing you with insights into your performance and identifying any inaccuracies or errors in the execution of tasks or actions undertaken by you.

If you deem it beneficial to proactively seek the assistance of a therapist, it is recommended that you schedule a consultation with your primary healthcare professional for guidance or a suitable referral. Occasionally, insurance policies may restrict coverage for therapy sessions unless accompanied by a referral, making this an approach to bypass said requirement. In addition, your physician will be able to ascertain any potential physiological factors contributing to the symptoms you are experiencing, specifically pertaining to your cardiovascular health. You possess just a solitary instance of this, nevertheless.

Upon receiving a referral for therapy, you may commence deliberating on the most suitable form of therapy to address your needs. Would you be interested in engaging the services of a cognitive behavioral therapist? Traditional talk therapy? Some other kind? There exist diverse modalities of therapy available for individuals experiencing anxiety, and ultimately, the selection of the approach to pursue will rest upon your personal discretion. Once you have reached a conclusion, it is recommended that you proceed by examining healthcare providers within your vicinity who either accept your insurance or offer services at a reasonable cost, should they not accept your insurance.

When you ultimately encounter your therapist, it is important to maintain a receptive attitude while also considering the necessity of establishing a rapport with the individual. It is crucial to ensure that you establish a sense of comfort with the individual you are engaging in conversation with. Nevertheless, in numerous cases, it proves challenging to make an accurate assessment based on a solitary session. It is advised to make an effort to schedule a minimum of two sessions with a therapist before concluding that they may not be a suitable match for your needs. It is imperative to ensure that the therapeutic process is genuinely effective by identifying a suitable match for you.

Simulation of the most unfavorable eventualities

Another strategy that individuals have found beneficial in effectively addressing anxiety is the practice of engaging in a roleplay exercise that involves envisioning and preparing for the most unfavorable outcome. In the present situation, you are presented with the task of envisioning the most unfavorable outcome pertaining to your underlying anxiety. For instance, in the event that you are experiencing apprehension regarding a potential divorce, you can engage in a contemplative process wherein you deliberate upon the hypothetical outcome of the most unfavorable circumstances, meticulously outlining the precise course of action that would ensue. It is possible that you have concerns about the potential outcome of your impending divorce, wherein your soon-to-be ex-spouse might obtain sole custody of the children as well as exclusive ownership of the property. This could leave you burdened with substantial child support obligations for children with whom you have limited contact. Moreover, there is the unfortunate possibility that your children may become estranged from you, resulting in a significant reduction or complete cessation of your interactions with them. Perhaps this scenario entails a progression wherein you forfeit any form of communication with your children and are reduced solely to serving as a financial provider for their activities, medical coverage, and other necessities, while your former spouse enters into a new marriage with an individual who assumes the parental role that you deeply desire.

Cease and enact that scenario. Subsequently, it is imperative to contemplate the level of feasibility. To what extent do parents frequently experience a complete breakdown in communication with their children, unless their actions are adversely impacting the well-being of the children? To what extent do instances arise where individuals who engage in substance abuse or mistreat their children maintain legal custody of their offspring? What is the probability of your former partner stopping, taking custody of the children, and fleeing? What could be the rationale behind your previous partner's inclination to engage in actions detrimental to the well-being of your children, who would undoubtedly thrive with the presence of both parents, assuming there is no mistreatment or disregard involved?

As you carefully analyze the circumstances, you begin to comprehend that the probability of your most unfavorable outcome materializing is highly remote. This realization provides a measure of solace, alleviating any lingering apprehension you may have about the matter and allowing you to proceed onward.

3. The Influence of Physical Contact

Massages have demonstrated considerable efficacy in ameliorating anxiety and enhancing one's psychological well-being. This phenomenon occurs due to the efficacy of a well-executed massage in inducing relaxation, thereby diminishing the secretion of cortisol, a hormone associated with stress, while simultaneously bolstering the release of serotonin and dopamine, neurotransmitters known for their mood-enhancing properties. These hormones and neurotransmitters play a pivotal role in the regulation of mood.

If the cost of a massage therapy is beyond your means, alternatively, you may seek the companionship of a friend, spouse, or close family member to provide gentle touch, which can effectively diminish your stress response and simultaneously decrease your blood pressure. Similarly, petting a furry animal can also give you the same touch benefits. This phenomenon can be attributed to the fact that engaging in affectionate physical contact with animals has demonstrated an elevation in the production of oxytocin hormone, a well-regarded substance recognized for its capacity to promote social bonding and enhance one's overall emotional state. Massage therapy is particularly efficacious in alleviating the symptoms associated with General Anxiety Disorder (GAD), which is widely recognized as the prevailing form of anxiety.

A beneficial massage can also facilitate the elimination of toxins. As an example, it has the potential to facilitate the decomposition of built-up toxins or waste within muscular tissues. Additionally, it possesses a commendable ability to alleviate anxiety in patients. During the course of a massage, it is advised to refrain from engaging in conversation or dedicating one's thoughts to personal subjects pertaining to family, work, or financial concerns. Alternatively, it is advisable to unwind and empty one's mind. Please bc aware that massage therapy requires a certain amount of time to effectively initiate its therapeutic effects. Therefore, in the event that you encounter enduring discomfort accompanied by tension, it might be necessary to undergo multiple sessions, and thus you should refrain from anticipating immediate outcomes.

If one wishes to combat anxiety, one may choose among the various available types of massage. Some of these include:

Deep Tissue massage – This modality has been specifically tailored to address the underlying layers of muscles and connective tissue. The professionals typically necessitate extensive training and exceptional comprehension of physiology and anatomy to execute this technique accurately.

The Swedish massage is a robust therapy specifically crafted to invigorate the body through the promotion of circulation. It encompasses the utilization of five fundamental techniques encompassing tapping, percussive, vibration, rolling, and kneading as a means of manipulating the soft tissues of the body.

4

9. Exercise

Physical activity plays a crucial role in enhancing cognitive well-being, while also serving as a potent tool in combatting feelings of stress and anxiety. Furthermore, it possesses the capacity to diminish weariness, heighten attentiveness and focus, while also augmenting cognitive capabilities. What is the connection between the two?

Exercise and various forms of physical activity typically enhance the synthesis of endorphins, the neurochemicals responsible for pain alleviation and sleep enhancement. Consequently, this fosters a decrease in anxiety levels.

Various scientific research has shown that partaking in consistent aerobic exercise can effectively diminish tension levels and enhance the mood, resulting in increased stability. Additionally, engaging in such exercises can contribute to enhancing both your sleep patterns and self-worth. Indeed, partaking in aerobic exercise for a mere five minutes can effectively elicit substantial anti-anxiety outcomes. Nevertheless, in order to fully maximize the advantages of physical activity, it is recommended to strive towards participating in one hour and fifteen minutes of vigorous-intensity exercises such as crunches and boxing, or two hours and thirty minutes of moderate-intensity physical activities per week, or even a blend of these two.

During the formulation of your exercise regimen, it is imperative to:

Establish daily goals that are Specific, Measurable, Achievable, Relevant, and Time-bound, and prioritize daily consistency over striving for perfection right from the beginning. Engaging in a daily 20-25 minute walk is considerably more beneficial and convenient compared to reserving a lengthy 3-hour fitness session exclusively for the weekend. Extensive research has consistently demonstrated that the frequency of occurrence holds greater significance than any other factor.

Discover forms of physical activity that offer pleasure. If the exercise does not bring about enjoyment, it is improbable that you will persist in engaging in it and probable that you will abandon it.

Find a partner. It is frequently more convenient to maintain regularity in your exercise regimen when you are accountable to a friend, companion, or associate.

Developing Authentic Self-Assurance As An Effective Measure Against Anxiety.

Are you aware of the distinction between confidence and competence? When you possess a sense of certainty, your expectations tend to be elevated. The elevated level of expectation may stem from various factors; nonetheless, regardless of the underlying cause, an individual harbors a steadfast belief in a favorable outcome with regard to a particular situation. With competence, one can be assured of possessing the requisite skills to effectively navigate a given situation, as attested by a proven track record. The issue inherent in solely relying on confidence lies in its potential for volatility. You are inclined to place a greater emphasis on competence. Consider it from this perspective. If I were to provide you with a glass of water, what would be the source of that water? Suppose I obtained it from a water filtration faucet, where the mechanism involves inverted five-gallon water containers. Now, from whence did that water originate? Suppose it originated from a rehabilitation facility. Now, from whence did that water originate? Suppose this originated from a certain river, somewhere? Now, from whence does that water originate? This epitomizes the essence of competence and stands as a paramount method to surmount anxiety. Perhaps it is possible that you have lacked sufficient exposure to situations in which you have emerged as the victor. It is possible that you have become habituated to situations unfolding unfavorably, leading doubt and apprehension to prevail as the prevailing forces in your emotional state. One can initiate the process by cultivating confidence, which entails formulating situations with elevated aspirations and progressively building upon them. However, even within this procedure, it is imperative to direct your attention towards the actions undertaken to actively construct these circumstances. It is imperative to recognize that acquiring knowledge of one's own identity and current capabilities (rather than focusing on future aspirations) is the most effective approach to placing oneself in advantageous situations that foster genuine personal growth and the development of confidence and competence. Anxiety is indicative of sentiments of uncertainty, concern, distress, fear, and skepticism. When one possesses both assurance and proficiency, they will perceive any manifestation of anxiety as a personal challenge that they are certain to overcome. It is imperative that you alter your perspective on certain aspects of your life. In a previous chapter, we have posited that the shift lies not in the mere rewiring of one's brain but rather in the alteration of one's perspective or lens through which something is viewed. By altering one's perspective, it becomes possible to modify the emanation of energy from an object or situation. As an illustration, I may experience a slight sense of apprehension when faced with the prospect of delivering a speech on a grand platform before an audience of

1000 individuals. Nonetheless, what if I were to adopt an alternative perspective? What if, instead of harboring concerns and uncertainties, I chose to perceive this as an opportunity for personal development at that particular instance? This entails having the courage to make mistakes on the stage, while maintaining a primary emphasis on the delivery of my words with an aim to achieve remarkable success. Recall the aforementioned adage "simply envision them clad in undergarments." There is a rationale behind why this statement would be expressed to an individual experiencing apprehension towards public speaking, as it proves to be effective. It may present challenges, however, it is imperative for one to adopt a reframed perspective by stepping back and acquiring a new outlook. Indeed, it is plausible that the individual you aspire to engage with may decline your advances; however, one can perceive this situation as an opportunity to receive constructive criticism and enhance oneself in the midst of this experience. You may utilize this opportunity to enhance your ability to engage with individuals of the opposite gender, thereby transforming the apprehension of rejection into a valuable opportunity for experiential learning. Are you able to perceive and comprehend the actions we have just taken?

Engaging In Physical Activity For Serenity And Relaxation

A frequently underestimated factor, particularly in the realm of managing and dealing with social anxiety or any other form of anxiety disorder, is the incorporation of physical exercise. Research has indicated that in addition to reducing the likelihood of cardiovascular conditions, such as heart disease, stroke, and high blood pressure, as well as metabolic disorders like diabetes and obesity, a consistent regimen of physical activity can also prove advantageous in the management of anxiety disorders, including social anxiety disorder and various other manifestations. Engaging in physical activity is an effective method for naturally alleviating anxiety and effectively managing levels of stress. Based on my own personal experiences, I can verify the veracity of this statement, or alternatively, my spouse can provide confirmation. After each workout session, I consistently experience a revitalizing effect, resulting in an enhanced emotional state.

Is there a correlation between exercise and physical activities?

A common misconception among individuals is that the two entities are indistinguishable. Therefore, if your assumption was in alignment, there is no need to feel remorseful or be burdened by it. You will not face legal repercussions for making such an assumption. Nevertheless, it can be argued that the dissimilarities between the two outweigh any shared characteristics. In addition to muscle contractions, the two exhibit notable dissimilarities.

When referring to physical activity, it encompasses any form of movement that induces muscle contraction. Anything. When one engages in the act of blinking one's eye, it can be considered a form of physical exercise. Engaging in the act of disposing of the garbage involves engaging in physical activity. Engaging in the act of eating entails the performance of physical activity.

Exercise is a distinct type of physical activity that stands apart due to its specificity and regulation. Physical activities vary in purpose, encompassing tasks such as domestic chores and meal preparation. In contrast, exercise is intentionally performed in order to enhance physical strength, stamina, and cardiovascular wellbeing, with specific consideration given to duration, intensity, and prescribed movements. Physical fitness endeavors encompass engaging in weightlifting using barbells and dumbbells within a gymnasium, participating in a 5-kilometer run on an athletic track, or indulging in swimming, among various alternative pursuits.

The significance of exercise possessing a highly systematic manifestation cannot be overstated. The observant reader may have discerned that the majority of the therapeutic approaches presented in this book for addressing Seasonal Affective Disorder (SAD) are characterized by systematic and well-timed methodologies. Engaging in physical exertion exhibits no variance. This kind of organization plays a crucial role in providing a framework for our lives, which holds immense significance for individuals who have experienced anxiety disorders. Given the prevailing ambiguity in the world, it is reassuring to acknowledge that one maintains a significant level of control over a particular aspect with utmost certainty.

Regarding the notion of intensity, it can be delineated as the level of exertion one applies in the execution of a given task. From a quantitative perspective in the context of physical activity, the measurement is designated by Metabolic Equivalents (METs). This pertains to the quotient obtained by dividing your metabolic rate during physical activity by your metabolic rate at rest or at baseline. One unit of metabolic equivalent of task (MET) is associated with an approximate energy expenditure of 1 calorie per kilogram of body weight per hour.

Various intensity levels exist in regards to exercise, typically categorized as light, moderate, or high intensity. There exists a highly technical, and may I add, intellectually inclined, approach to quantifying your present level of exercise intensity. However, it goes without saying that allocating precious time for such endeavors may not be the most expeditious use of one's resources. A straightforward yet effective method for gauging your current exercise intensity is by utilizing the talk test.

The procedure for the talk test is as follows. During physical activity, aim to engage in conversation. If one is able to engage in conversation effortlessly, it indicates that they are engaging in physical activity at a low intensity level. If one retains the ability to communicate clearly with moderate exertion, then the exercise intensity can be deemed as moderate. If one finds it extremely arduous to converse and experiences great difficulty in taking in adequate breaths, such a state may be regarded as indicative of high intensity. The degree of variation in these levels will significantly differ among individuals, primarily contingent on their physical condition, age, and other pertinent factors. If two individuals are performing the identical exercise in close proximity, one may be experiencing significant shortness of breath while the other appears to be exerting minimal effort. I apologize for the play on words, but do not worry if you do not possess the same level of fitness as others. The crucial aspect is to ascertain one's individual exercise thresholds, without any further additions. Undoubtedly, with the enhancement of stamina, there will be a corresponding adjustment in the levels.

Optimal Intensity for Effective Anxiety Management

In terms of managing and dealing with your social anxiety, the most suitable level of exercise intensity would be classified as moderate. Why? An insufficient level of intensity fails to yield significant results, such as effective weight loss, which plays a paramount role in enhancing one's self-esteem and subsequently alleviating social anxiety.

Exerting excessive effort can be counterproductive, as it may intensify stress levels by depleting your energy reserves and potentially exacerbate symptoms of anxiety. Given your objective of effectively addressing and overseeing your social anxiety, it is essential to avoid experiencing additional stress and associated manifestations of anxiety, correct? Right!

Engaging in moderate physical activity for a minimum duration of 30 minutes, three times per week, is considered optimal. It is not excessively effortless to yield substantial influence nor excessively taxing to exacerbate your preexisting anxiety concerns. Briefer time intervals are less conducive, as they provide insufficient duration to elevate your heart rate and establish a steady exercise tempo.

Some of the additional techniques that have been previously discussed in this book can also be integrated with physical activity to achieve peak performance. During the process of physical exertion, one has the opportunity to assess their thought patterns either verbally or silently. An additional technique that you could employ is diaphragmatic breathing. Engaging in yoga postures before and after engaging in moderate physical activity can also be beneficial, while concluding the session with a session focused on muscle relaxation can provide an added advantage.

Anxiety and Relationships

In contrast to the depictions in countless romantic comedies, it should be noted that achieving a state of everlasting joy does not occur effortlessly. Although it is inherent for humans to seek companionship and establish meaningful connections with others, the ability to maintain wholesome relationships can be developed through acquired knowledge and expertise. From an early age, we begin to explore avenues for establishing connections with those in our immediate vicinity. We acquire the skills of cooperation, develop a sense of compassion, and exhibit benevolence towards our fellow human beings.

Extensive research has revealed that the inherent drive to establish connections with others is intrinsic. This implies that solitude is not inherent to our nature. We possess an inherent longing for companionship, hence seeking the assurance provided by a steadfast relationship. Connections between individuals offer a sense of security and establish a sanctuary where we can freely express ourselves, fostering an enriched existence through the companionship of another.

As a young individual, your affection and loyalty towards individuals in your vicinity are consistently unwavering. During our youth, we tend to believe and adhere to the teachings of our parents or caregivers due to our limited exposure to alternative perspectives. Despite the disciplinary actions taken by your parents, you persist in seeking solace from them as they represent the most crucial emotional bond in your life during your childhood.

As we transition into the realm of adulthood, the veil of innocence is gradually lifted, rendering relationships increasingly complex. Based on the nature of the relationships you experienced during your early years, you are likely to carry a significant amount of adverse emotional burdens into adulthood. It is possible that the individual's codependency stems from a challenging upbringing or presents itself through personality attributes such as narcissism. Irrespective of the emotional burdens one carries, it is undeniably evident that they exert a profound influence on the nature of one's interpersonal connections in adulthood.

Individuals with codependency tendencies often have an inherent reliance on consistent validation from others in order to maintain a positive self-perception. This particular form of adverse attachment emerges during early childhood, contributing to the development of characteristics such as narcissism and avoidant personality. Take into account the situation of a young child who is perpetually subjected to parental criticism and derogatory remarks. The more they are subjected to criticism, the stronger their desire becomes to receive approval from their parents. This implies that the child's primary focus will be directed towards seeking validation and approval from their parent.

As this child matures into adulthood, it is highly probable that they will continue to possess the need for validation from others. This is frequently attributed to the significant portion of brain development that takes place during infancy; consequently, the characteristics acquired during toddlerhood tend to become firmly embedded in one's personality.

In the majority of instances, these attributes acquired during childhood will significantly influence your interpersonal connections. You will observe that your relationships follow a uniform path and eventually converge at a common destination. A significant number of individuals who experience a string of unsuccessful relationships often perceive that they are engaging in a comparable relationship repeatedly. In the event that they are incapable of discerning the emotional burden that is impeding their capacity to form successful interpersonal connections, their prospects of cultivating fulfilling relationships are minimal.

In instances where individuals encounter difficulties in developing mutually beneficial emotional connections, the presence of anxiety often becomes a fundamental characteristic within their interpersonal relationships. You consistently experience apprehension regarding the potential failure of your relationship or the prospect of your partner abandoning you. You frequently doubt your own value and consistently anticipate unfavorable outcomes. This particular form of intense emotional disturbance not only inflicts psychological harm upon the individual, but it also exerts pressure on the dynamics of the relationship.

The presence of anxiety in relationships is typically instigated by an incapacity to establish positive interpersonal connections. This implies that you lack the ability to maintain a mutually balanced and healthy relationship. Either an individual may discern the need to govern the actions of another person, or they may perceive that if circumstances do not unfold in a particular manner, calamity is inevitable. You initiate a process of suffocation upon your partner, and subsequently, you gradually alienate them due to the depletion of all pleasure within the relationship.

Other Tips

Day 19: Foster proactive thinking

At this point in time, you have become acquainted with the factors that elicit anxiety within you. If one encounters specific triggers, it is imperative to promptly recognize them and make diligent efforts to prevent the exacerbation of anxiety symptoms. This necessitates the need for strategic planning.

Commence by acquiring the ability to identify the indications of anxiety. The more promptly you identify them, the earlier you can initiate efforts to eliminate them. Subsequently, delineate a list of actions that can be implemented promptly in order to regain control when one becomes aware of the encroachment of anxiety. Undoubtedly, you have already acquired knowledge regarding techniques to alleviate the mental distress caused by anxiety. However, the ease of accomplishing immediate relief varies depending on your location. For instance, the practice of engaging in deep breathing exercises can be conducted effortlessly irrespective of location or timing, thereby aiding in alleviating accompanying symptoms. Additionally, should you find yourself in a situation where you are awaiting the arrival of someone or something, you might consider procuring your mobile device and engaging in the pursuit of a puzzle game, which could prove to be a more convenient option. However, indulging in activities such as enjoying a hot bath may need to be delayed until your return to your place of residence.

An additional aspect that can be beneficial is envisioning your response to various circumstances. Devise a hypothetical situation and subsequently ascertain your planned response to it. Ensure that you consider a variety of scenarios and anticipate a range of potential outcomes. This will instill in your mind the ability to anticipate and adapt to both positive and negative outcomes. It will demonstrate that irrespective of circumstances, life continues to progress, necessitating the need to responsibly address and navigate through them, rather than becoming fixated within a specific moment.

Day 20: Engage in a Period of Digital Abstinence

The subsequent step you must take entails engaging in a period of digital detoxification. Technological advancements have undeniably facilitated the facilitation of communication processes and enhanced the accessibility of information.

Nevertheless, this does not always prove advantageous. If you find yourself consistently allocating an extensive amount of time engaging in conversations with unfamiliar individuals or indulging in the dissemination of idle rumors, it would be advisable to reduce indulgence in such activities. Upon your arrival at home, refrain from verifying any work-related updates. It is advisable for you to acquire the skill of effectively compartmentalizing your professional and personal spheres. It is imperative to develop the ability to separate oneself from individuals with whom one has incompatible dispositions. Please retrieve a telephone device and initiate the process of removing contact information. Examine your social media profiles and ascertain your true objectives for engaging with them. There is no necessity for you to allocate several hours to engage in social media activities. It fails to enhance one's emotional state. There is a correlation between frequent smartphone usage and increased levels of stress and anxiety among individuals. Give yourself a break.

Additionally, it is advisable to reduce your consumption of television programs. Furthermore, this encompasses your consumption of news programs. Contemporary news and entertainment programs are replete with disheartening imagery. It is unnecessary to consistently expose oneself to such scenes while seeking tranquility. If your desire is to be entertained, select a performance that instills a sense of positivity. In summary, it is advisable to reduce the duration of digital media usage overall.

Methodology Used In Cognitive Behavioral Therapy.

Prior to delving into the intricacies of Cognitive Behavioral Therapy (CBT), it is crucial to contemplate the objectives you aspire to attain through addressing your anxiety. In order to establish objectives, it is imperative to first analyze the fundamental concerns associated with anxiety and the precise manifestations experienced. Every individual has a distinctive array of concerns, even if they share an anxiety diagnosis.

Anne is seated in a hunched posture at her desk, her head cradled by her hands. A conscientious colleague discreetly makes physical contact with her by tapping her shoulder. Have you been feeling well? It seems that colleagues have previously observed her appearing tense. In professional circles, she is renowned for her tendency to be overly concerned.

Although Anne exhibits exceptional performance in her professional role, her incessant apprehensiveness hampers her daily approach. Is it probable that I will arrive tardy this morning?" "Is there a possibility that I will face termination?" "In the event of illness or if my husband were to experience job loss, what plan of action would be employed to manage our expenses?" "How will our financial obligations be met?" "In the unfortunate event that my children sustain injuries, what measures would be implemented to address such situations?" Continuously recurring thoughts of this nature persistently pervade her mind, impeding her ability to focus and complete tasks.

Anne experiences fatigue as a result of her frequent migraines, bodily discomfort, and sleeplessness. Her spouse is also growing increasingly impatient with her. As a result of her frequent late work shifts, their communication has substantially diminished.

Recognizing Anne's evident distress, the supervisor proactively connects her with the Employee Assistance Program (EAP) at their disposal. Via the Employee Assistance Program, she engages in sessions with a therapist, wherein they collectively address the challenges she has been experiencing. Anne discovers that her symptoms align with the characteristics of generalized anxiety disorder.

She communicates to her therapist that she harbors the belief that her anxiety is persistent and unlikely to diminish in the future. The therapist comprehends the client's concerns and provides reassurance, highlighting his previous achievements in employing short-term cognitive behavioral therapy for clients facing comparable anxieties. They devise a strategy to convene for a total of seven successive sessions, subsequently assessing her advancement.

Developing Familiarity with Your Anxiety

Which symptoms of your anxiety are the most bothersome to you? In what aspects of your life has anxiety made the greatest impact? Delineating your distinct symptoms and determining the specific areas in which assistance is necessary constitutes a crucial aspect in elucidating your objectives.

Please pause to document your emotions. Are there certain aspects of your life that you believe require the utmost consideration? What specific manifestations of anxiety pose the greatest challenges in your daily life? Please reflect upon a recent incidence that triggered feelings of anxiety and record notable aspects of the situation that have made a significant impression on your thoughts.

1. Previous: The Genesis of Social Anxiety

Several theories exist regarding the etiology of social anxiety disorder. Each individual possesses unique attributes and is apt to harbor distinctive stimuli. Elements such as one's upbringing, cultural background, and experiences marked by trauma can each exert a significant influence. In the following discourse, I shall present an analysis of the prevailing factors contributing to individuals experiencing social anxiety.

Behavioral

There exists a theoretical proposition positing that certain individuals may acquire a social anxiety disorder as a consequence of previous experiences. It is a well-established fact that when a child comes into contact with a hot object, such as an oven door, they acquire a firsthand experience of the pain that ensues. As a result, they inevitably internalize the knowledge that oven doors should be evaded due to their propensity to cause harm and inflict injuries. Likewise, instances of social settings where you expcrienced humiliation, embarrassment, or fearfulness could potentially impact your emotional state in subsequent social circumstances. It is possible that you harbor apprehension concerning the likelihood of similar situations, leading you to actively avoid them.

Evidently, there are several issues associated with this theory. For behavioral psychology to be effective, it is imperative to ensure the presence of a recurring event. Consequently, to establish a correlation between all social situations and a sense of unease, one would inevitably need to experience recurring instances of embarrassing circumstances. Although there is a possibility that certain individuals may have disproportionately higher instances of socially humiliating experiences, it would require a significant degree of misfortune for behavioral psychology to be applicable in this context.

Thinking

An alternative hypothesis suggests that certain individuals possess a cognitive orientation that predisposes them to develop social anxiety. An individual experiencing social anxiety tends to anticipate their own underperformance and perceive a constant scrutiny from others. Individuals affected by social anxiety tend to harbor doubts regarding their capacity to assimilate and participate in social settings, perceiving themselves as uninteresting and assuming that their opinions hold no value to others. Thought processes such as these tend to amplify ordinary feelings of anxiety, transforming them into something more severe.

Individuals demonstrating this mindset are frequently referred to as worrywarts or individuals with a tendency to exhibit pessimistic attitudes. These individuals seldom adopt an optimistic perspective and consistently dwell on potential adversities instead. Certain individuals may exhibit a propensity for engaging in this type of thinking to a greater extent than others, however, it is frequently a cognitive pattern that is acquired rather than innate. This is certainly positive news as it indicates that you can effectively undergo a successful transformation in your thinking patterns.

Day 1

Exercise:

Locate a secluded area devoid of any disturbances, and power down all electronic devices. Assume an upright posture with your back aligned, assume a kneeling position, or recline on a firm surface (excluding a bed) while observing a period of silence lasting 10 minutes.

Throughout this 10-minute duration, engage in deliberate and deep inhalations, retaining the breath momentarily before releasing. Exhale slowly. Pay close attention to the sound and rhythm of your breath. Do not attempt to alter the situation; instead, adopt an attitude of attentive receptiveness and experience the inhalation and exhalation of the air.

Once you feel prepared, please proceed to recite the following mantra: "Remain in a state of tranquility." Maintain silence. Reiterate this instruction slowly, both audibly and in a subdued manner, multiple times. One may encounter feelings of ennui or unease, yet it is essential to persist in reciting the mantra without cessation. Continuously practice it until you attain a state of tranquility and concentration. One may choose to sustain the deep breathing technique while reciting the mantra, or alternatively, engage in deep breaths during moments of silence. Don't rush.

Every single one of the thirty days will encompass a period of silence, concentrated breathing, and the recitation of a mantra. With the exception of this page, each day's conclusion will serve as a reminder of the moments devoted to moments of stillness and deliberate contemplative breathing, along with the inclusion of a mantra for your practice. You have the option to recite the mantras either during your periods of silence and focused breathing or subsequently. Please be reminded that there is no definitive or incorrect approach in achieving this task.

Negative thoughts and emotions are inclined to engage in conflict; in fact, they thrive on confrontation. Rather than engaging in a battle with anxiety, approach it with calmness and attentiveness. Allow the exercises and lessons within this program to serve as your guiding force.

Please consider sharing your experience by utilizing the hashtag #30DaysBreathing.

Day 2

Exercise:

Consider this inquiry: Have you ever experienced a moment in your life where you were entirely devoid of any sense of anxiety?

Writing has significant advantages for the cognitive faculties, particularly during moments of contemplation. Please articulate your reflections on this specific inquiry. In the event that your thoughts become diverted, proceed to document any ensuing reflections. It is acceptable if you do not have anything to write, yet I urge you to contemplate the question nonetheless.

Have you been able to recall a time in your life during which you were not encountering feelings of anxiety? If you belong to the majority of individuals, you may find it necessary to draw upon recollections from your early years to ascertain that specific timeframe. It is quite commonplace for an individual to encounter anxiety in their formative years and persistently grapple with it throughout their lifespan. From a young age, we are instilled with apprehension towards upcoming events both in educational and familial contexts, consequently fostering the development of a bond with anxiety. The majority of individuals are instructed to be excessively sensitive regarding occurrences or non-occurrences; nevertheless, it is not imperative to maintain an attachment to these anxious cognitive patterns.

Acknowledge that anxiety is a acquired misconception with underlying origins. Nevertheless, it can be swiftly and entirely relinquished, and you possess the capacity to do so. Put simply, you are not under the sway, recognition, or subjugation of an acquired misapprehension regarding forthcoming encounters. This is a misleading perception that you no longer need to endure; it is now opportune to let it be. Anxiety is a learned response that possesses the potential for unlearning.

*A period of 10 minutes dedicated to stillness and intentional deep breathing. Repeat the mantra: "Drop. Unlearn. Discover."

(Please feel free to document and discuss this experience using the designated hashtag #30DaysPonder)

8 Efficacious Strategies for the Management of Anger

Rage forms an integral component of the full spectrum of human emotions. It is healthy. We can experience anger if there exists a valid cause for such an emotion. Nevertheless, there are occasions when it becomes arduous to exercise control. Unrestrained or unchecked rage can give rise to a tendency that poses challenges or difficulties. Fortuitously, as mentioned by clinical psychologist Isabel Clarke, it is within your power to manage and regulate your anger, and it is incumbent upon you to fulfill this obligation.

Rage encompasses among the most potent human sentiments. Exerting control over it can present difficulties. Please find below a set of practical recommendations that can be employed when one experiences feelings of anger.

Anger management techniques

Isabel Clarke brings forth a word of caution regarding anger: "Each individual inevitably experiences a response to anger." Pay attention to the signals your body is sending and implement measures to achieve a state of tranquility.

This implies that anger exhibits a discernible pattern. You are cognizant of the triggers that prompt anger within you and possess an awareness of the circumstances under which you are likely to become angry. Given your ability to anticipate your own behavior, designing an action plan may prove to be a straightforward task. Allow me to suggest some actions you may consider taking.

1. Exercise caution in recognizing indicators of anger

You are aware of the indications that denote anger. An accelerated respiration rate and an increased heart rate manifest. It appears that you are experiencing tension in your jaw and your hands are tightly closed. This would imply that you are on the verge of executing a highly destructive course of action. According to Isabel Clarke, it is advised that individuals with a history of losing control should remove themselves from the situation if they observe these indicators.

Occasionally, the act of evading can prove to be the most efficient course of action. Do not postpone addressing the management of your emotions until you reach a state of incapacity. Please expedite your response at the earliest convenience.

2. Enumerate from 1 to 10.

Although it may appear amusing, it can prove to be advantageous. Numerating up to ten aids in the postponement of one's actions. Furthermore, it assists in the precise and constructive assessment of the potential consequences resulting from your actions.

3. Regulate your breath at a slower pace.

Slowing down your breath is regarded as one of the most efficient techniques for managing anger effectively. Indeed, by exercising control over one's breath, one has the capacity to exercise control over one's temper. Isabel further remarked, "It is worth mentioning that during moments of anger, one tends to inhale more than exhale. The key lies in exhaling more than inhaling." This will serve to effectively ensure your tranquility and enhance your cognitive clarity.

4. Exercise

An alternative approach to efficiently manage your anger is to participate in physical pursuits, such as engaging in regular exercise. Engaging in activities such as walking, jogging, swimming, and participating in outdoor sports can be efficacious in temper reduction. Isabel Clarke asserts that incorporating exercise into one's daily routine is an effective method for alleviating irritation and anger.

5. Ensure your well-being.

Irritation can occasionally arise from a confluence of heightened tension and a lack of concern for oneself. You are engaged in attending to the needs of others, inadvertently neglecting your own needs. Therefore, taking care of oneself can result in a state of tranquility. Perhaps it would be advantageous to embark on a vacation and partake in a period of relaxation. Ensure you obtain sufficient amount of rest and refrain from the consumption of substances such as drugs, caffeine, and alcohol. These chemicals are influential factors in the development of stress. Indeed, Isabel Clarke asserts that "They diminish inhibitions and, in reality, inhibitions are necessary to prevent us from behaving inappropriately when experiencing anger."

6. Make something interesting

Engaging in hobbies can serve as a valuable means to alleviate your anger. One potential method of anger management that has proven to be effective is engaging in creative outlets such as writing, dancing, painting, singing, and composing music. These activities serve to mitigate feelings of anger and alleviate bodily tension.

7. Express your feeling

Expressing your emotions to others can prove beneficial in alleviating the weight of your emotional load. Moreover, it is of utmost significance that you engage additional individuals in devising efficacious solutions.

8. Liberate your mind from any thoughts that provoke anger.

Occasionally, feelings of anger stem from cognitive processes within your mind. If one continues to dwell on the unfavorable nature of a situation, it becomes difficult to overcome it. Hence, according to Isabel Clarke, it is recommended to endeavor to relinquish any counterproductive cognitive patterns. Ideas such as "The situation lacks fairness" or "Individuals of such nature should not be given access to the roads" can exacerbate feelings of anger.

In order to emancipate yourself from any pessimistic thoughts, endeavor to refrain from employing the subsequent expressions:

I've noticed a consistent lack of receptivity to my input.

It is imperative for me to arrive punctually.

The world possesses inherent inequities.

I kindly request that you consistently adhere to my preferences.

Four: Examining Nonverbal Communication

Gaining insight into the thoughts and emotions of others commences with the observation of nonverbal cues. The investigation commences by observing individuals' conduct and discerning the non-verbal cues emanating from their bodies, irrespective of the spoken language. Nonverbal communication, despite its more primitive nature compared to explicit verbal expression of thoughts and emotions, remains equally efficacious. In fact, nonverbal cues have been harnessed by nature throughout countless millennia across various species. Social animals, as a collective, engage in nonverbal communication, utilizing a variety of distinct methods to effectively convey their messages. Even bees have a complex form of communication through their movements that allow other bees to know where they need to go.

Nonverbal communication constitutes the majority of all interpersonal communication, underscoring its utmost significance for both utilization and comprehension. It is imperative that you acquire an understanding of this matter in order to gain insight into the underlying proceedings. Due to this rationale, we shall allocate this to the examination of nonverbal communication, the key elements to consider while attempting comprehension, and techniques for interpreting it. Regarding the ability to interpret individuals, one should focus on their body language and gestures.

Defining Nonverbal Communication

In essence, nonverbal communication can be succinctly described as the means through which your body engages in communicative acts devoid of verbal expression. This implies that it occurs in the absence of verbal communication. Nevertheless, there is a deeper dimension to the subject at hand—nonverbal communication operates on an unconscious level. When engaging in nonverbal communication, your body will generate cues that are transmitted to individuals in your vicinity. The individuals in your vicinity are subsequently capable of perceiving and deciphering the signals you emit, leading to their comprehension and interpretation.

Your verbal interactions with individuals encompass more than just the literal expression of words; there are additional elements involved. The subtle gestures you make are unconsciously perceived and understood by those in your vicinity. This is the reason why individuals experience intuitive hunches about others during conversations. If you have previously experienced the sensation of discerning untruthfulness while conversing with someone, it is likely that you have encountered this impression. You are likely familiar with the sensation—a sense of being in a precarious situation wherein someone poses a potential threat or presents difficulties in various ways. Similarly, one can observe their amicability on such occasions. Recognizing the essentiality of comprehending nonverbal communication, as the mind instinctively interprets it. One can discern whether someone is posing a threat irrespective of their cultural background. One can discern the expression of joy from an individual, irrespective of their cultural background or geographical origin. This is because we possess a collective ability to interpret and comprehend body language that exhibits striking resemblances. It is understood that specific actions exhibit aggression, even in their inherent nature. Your physical being is cognizant of this, as is the case with your mental faculties, and your subconscious mind actively ensures that it encompasses all aspects of this experience.

Certainly, it is crucial to acknowledge that nonverbal communication can serve as a substitute for vocal expressions as well. Examples of vocal expressions such as groaning or sighing involve the production of sounds devoid of linguistically formed words. That fact alone renders it nonverbal. Verbal communication entails the utilization of language in various modalities, ranging from written expression to oral articulation. Hence, nonverbal communication encompasses all other forms of conveying information or messages. In the absence of verbal discourse, it can be attributed to nonverbal communication. Once one begins to acknowledge nonverbal communication as constituting the majority of our interchanges, one truly comprehends its remarkable influence.

Key Aspects to Consider in Nonverbal Communication

When it pertains to the ability to interpret nonverbal communication, there exist several straightforward aspects worth considering when observing it in others. Each of the different kinds of nonverbal communication becomes imperative for you to be able to discuss. The various manifestations of nonverbal communication that warrant your attention include kinesics, oculesics, haptics, proxemics, and vocalics.

Kinesics

Kinesics pertains to the overall nonverbal communication conveyed through bodily movements and gestures, exhibited in any given moment. It comprises the gestures, overall demeanor, and mannerisms exhibited by one's physical form. This concept is centered around kinesthetic stimulation, specifically pertaining to the element of physical motion. With this consideration in mind, it becomes effortless to maintain awareness of its nature. The majority of what you will acquire the ability to comprehend within this book primarily pertains to kinesics, primarily attributable to the significant prevalence of kinesic elements that contribute to the interpretation of nonverbal bodily cues.

Oculesics

Oculesics pertains to the intricate ocular gestures and movements. Although it can be considered a form of kinesics from a technical standpoint, its distinct focus necessitates separate evaluation and analysis. It encompasses the capacity to comprehend various ocular motions, spanning from the act of opening and closing eyes to the act of fixating upon objects, and beyond. It is essential to comprehend this concept in order to ensure your ability to interpret the eyes, often regarded as the windows to the soul.

Haptics

Haptics enables the utilization of tactile sensations to facilitate communication. Diverse tactile perceptions can effectively convey varied ideas, particularly in light of the extensive range of touch experiences. The act of physical contact can manifest in various forms, ranging from a gentle means of encouragement to a means of repulsion or even aggressive retaliation against another individual. Even a fleeting tactile interaction possesses the potential to convey significant information, and thus warrants careful contemplation.

Proxemics

Proxemics pertains to the utilization of spatial arrangements to convey various subjects or ideas. It can exhibit both vertical and horizontal orientations, in relation to one's positioning in relation to another individual. When considering proxemics, one examines how an employer might may seek to assert dominance over an individual being reprimanded, or how someone disinterested in another person may maintain a greater physical distance from them.

Vocalics

Ultimately, vocalics pertains to the manner in which one employs their vocalization to convey messages in a nonverbal manner. It encompasses interpersonal communication, social behavior, and vocal expression. Expressions of laughter, groaning, sighing, screeching, humming, and various related vocalizations serve as instances of nonverbal communication, enabling individuals to effectively convey messages to others.

The collective impact of these factors contributes to the formation of your nonverbal communication, rendering them essential to take into account. All of these factors are essential for enhancing your comprehension and potential ability to exert influence on others. We are dedicated to cultivating our skills in deciphering this information. Nonverbal communication plays a pivotal role in overall communication, and in its absence, one cannot expect to comprehend the complete context conveyed during interpersonal interactions. One will lack the ability to comprehend the true essence of things when one is unable to effectively communicate or perceive the underlying nuances. It is imperative to possess the ability to grasp and interpret the subtleties present in order to ensure a comprehensive comprehension of the situation at hand.

Therapy Using Cognitive Behavior

What is CBT?

The way we carry ourselves is highly influenced by the importance we place on our mental well-being. This is precisely why CBT (Cognitive Behavioral Therapy) endeavors to alter our cognitive processes, including ingrained beliefs that impede our progress, our perspectives on life's various challenges, and our behavioral responses when confronted with adversity, all while remaining focused on accomplishing our predetermined goals.

The process of modifying pessimistic thoughts through this therapeutic approach does not necessarily have to encompass your entire lifespan. Individuals who receive this treatment from their therapists are aware that the required duration is a minimum of ten months, with each session lasting 50-60 minutes and occurring once a week. Although we may consider it to be an interactive method necessitating both parties' presence, the experience of witnessing you manage your thoughts while being observed by someone constantly checking the time can occasionally be overwhelming.

Henceforth, we present to you a viable solution that can be implemented in the comfort of your own domicile.

It is imperative that professional assistance not be disregarded when it is made available. If you possess the ability to comprehend written text and have the capacity to discern the nature of your mental distress, it is conceivable that repeated visits to a serene location on a regular basis, akin to the therapeutic process, may obviate the requirement for professional therapeutic intervention.

A Brief Historical Account of Cognitive Behavioral Therapy

Aaron Beck is the renowned figure responsible for the development of this particular therapeutic approach. During the 1960s, this individual was actively engaged in the practice of psychoanalysis with his patients. While conducting the analysis, he observed a peculiar and atypical occurrence. It appeared that they were engaged in introspective contemplation, as if they were receiving inner messages or engaging in internal self-dialogue. When Beck inquired about their cognitive status, the patients provided only a fraction of the complete information.

For instance, it is likely that the individual receiving treatment within the therapist's premises was musing, "Today, the therapist appears unusually reticent." Could it be that my conversation is uninteresting to him, or is he preoccupied with deep contemplation? The initial thought prompted the subsequent inquiry, marking the beginning of this introspective dialogue. After a certain period of time, the client may begin to contemplate, "Perhaps my concerns do not hold significant importance to this individual of esteemed stature." At this juncture, they will fail to effectively convey their genuine emotions.

That was the moment when Beck gained the understanding that there exists a correlation between one's emotions and cognition. He proceeded to coin the term 'automatic thoughts' to denote the thoughts that are spontaneously generated in one's mind, devoid of the victim's conscious awareness, due to being inundated by emotions. Although clients may not possess direct insight into the workings of their brain, there exists a method to ascertain and chronicle these occurrences.

Through the identification of these cognitive patterns, the individual would subsequently gain insight into their internal state and gradually surmount the challenges encountered in one's life journey.

This marked the inception of Cognitive Behavioral Therapy. The main objective was to prioritize the significance of critical thinking in addressing our issues. The concepts of cognition and behavior are interconnected, as behavioral strategies must be considered alongside mental processes. The equilibrium between these two factors is subject to variation, contingent upon alternative therapeutic modalities that employ cognitive behavioral therapy as their central foundation; however, all such approaches fall within the scope of this treatment paradigm.

Presently, the field has been subject to numerous rigorous examinations conducted internationally with the aim of addressing issues pertaining to cognition and human behavior.

CBT in Depth

Cognitive Behavioral Therapy is an objective-focused psychological intervention that employs a proactive methodology aimed at resolving issues. The aim is to alter our cognitive patterns or the behavioral elements that give rise to the challenges, thereby substituting the center of our emotions. Upon reviewing the introduction, it becomes evident that this therapeutic approach encompasses a wide range of issues that can be effectively addressed, spanning from sleep disturbances to anxiety, depression, and substance dependency.

Employing cognitive behavioral therapy (CBT) involves facilitating a transformation in the individual's perspective and response to various circumstances through illuminating the cognitive processes that influence their beliefs, mental images, and thoughts. In this manner, the individual can channel their attention and effectively navigate emotionally charged circumstances.

Consider it as a synthesis of behavioral therapy and psychotherapy. The latter concerns itself with the significance we attribute to our life experiences and examines the origins of our thought processes from a young age. In contrast, behavioral therapy explores the intricate connection between our cognitive processes, personal issues, and behavioral patterns.

The subsequent diagram will illustrate the interconnectedness of the aforementioned elements. We will subsequently direct our attention towards it by illustrating similar patterns through the application of diverse real-life scenarios, mirroring the one portrayed below.

SCENARIO

CBT Principles

As it encompasses the acquisition of indispensable skills that equip us in coping with our emotional distress, embarking upon this journey shall bestow upon you novel approaches in conduct and cognition, enabling you to effectively regulate your circumstances moving forward. Below are several key aspects that must be comprehended prior to utilizing CBT.

This modality of therapy centers its attention on the current moment.

In order to elucidate the underlying cause of our current circumstances, it is imperative that we delve into our historical records. In contrast, the CBT therapy will prioritize the current symptoms that are leading you astray, rather than delving into the origins of the issue. For instance, in the case of anxiety, merely identifying its origin is insufficient to facilitate effective coping mechanisms.

Homework is Essential

Regardless of whether it is recommended by a therapist or prescribed in a self-help book, completing assigned tasks outside of therapy sessions is crucial. Completing the assigned tasks entails regular engagement and the continuous application of acquired skills on a daily basis. As this assignment pertains to your academic obligations, it is imperative that you diligently apply the knowledge acquired until it becomes deeply ingrained in your memory.

Merely recognizing the necessity of practice is insufficient; therefore, an additional factor beyond motivation is required. If you do not apply the knowledge you have acquired, it is highly probable that you will eventually forget it. When you confront your problem at a later time, it may prove challenging to recall how to effectively employ your acquired skills.

Acquiring proficiency in the novel techniques can be likened to the cultivation of a new behavior, specifically one that is conducive to well-being.

If the need arises for you to embark on a morning jogging routine, albeit initially challenging, persistence will ultimately render it habitual. Cognitive Behavioral Therapy employs the identical concept. By regularly engaging in the practice of behaviors that promote cognitive and behavioral change, one will quickly become accustomed to them. As one becomes more immersed in this practice, the subsequent progress becomes more effortless.

Are You Feeling Stressed? The Symptoms Revealed

The way you experience stress and anxiety will markedly vary from that of others. The level of distress experienced by an individual can vary significantly, with something that proves to be overwhelmingly intolerable for one person being a matter of minimal concern to another. How can one determine if the experienced emotional state truly corresponds to stress and anxiety, or if it is merely a consequence of a series of unfavorable circumstances?

There is, in fact, a minimal distinction separating the two - merely a couple of unfavorable days can swiftly escalate into a complete tempest. The sporadic instances of diminished self-assurance or unfavorable internal dialogue have the potential to rapidly amplify into a significant burden of anxiety. For this very reason, it is imperative to promptly recognize and address one's stress and anxiety before succumbing to pessimism and losing sight of one's aspirations and ambitions. In the event that you wish to apprehend it prior to it reaching an irreversible state, it is imperative for you to possess a clear understanding of the specific signs and indicators. This is the reason I have compiled an extensive inventory of numerous manifestations that one may observe while enduring chronic stress or anxiety. This encompasses both the immediate indications as well as the enduring, persistent symptoms.

Upon perusing the ensuing compilation, you may perceive a resemblance between yourself and a multitude of these symptoms, while remaining oblivious to their interconnectedness. Indeed, I did - and upon doing so, all the pieces fell into alignment and I was ultimately able to navigate through the situation.

Without any additional delay, let us now examine the symptoms at hand. Which symptoms are you able to identify?

Short-Term Symptoms (Acute Stress)

The following are the indicative symptoms that may manifest immediately subsequent to enduring a challenging circumstance. They are highly conspicuous, and they arise from the body's immediate physiological reaction to stress.

- Increased heart rate
- Superficial and accelerated respiration
- Sweating
- Heart palpitations
- Feeling faint
- Dry mouth
- Sensations of nervousness or unease in the abdomen • Experiencing a fluttering sensation in the stomach • Feeling a slight agitation or butterflies in the stomach
- Chest pains

- Hot flashes
- Headaches and migraines
- Loss of appetite
- Confusion
- Regularly experiencing the need to void one's bladder
- Feeling shaky
- Feeling sick
- Imagining doom
- Inability to relax

"Persistent Symptoms (Prolonged Stress)

There is a multitude of symptoms that frequently go unaddressed in regards to discussions surrounding stress and anxiety. Specifically, these symptoms pertain to the long-term consequences that occur as a cumulative effect of chronic stress endured over an extended duration. Examples of such symptoms may include unemployment, bereavement, and similar circumstances.

This inventory presented me with a comprehensive understanding of the complete magnitude of my problem. How about you?

- Experiencing persistent feelings of concern or unease
- Unable to concentrate
- Irritability
- Persistently experiencing a sense of unease or inability to unwind
- Feeling tearful
- Panic attacks
- High blood pressure
- Cephalalgia and persistent migraines
- Low self-esteem
- Adverse internal dialogue
- Seeking regular validation from others
- Requiring constant affirmation from others • Relying on frequent reassurance from others • Depending on regular validation from others • Seeking constant affirmation and reassurance from others
- Alopecia (telogen effluvium) • Thinning or shedding of hair (telogen effluvium) • Hair weakening and loss

(telogen effluvium) • Excessive hair fall (telogen effluvium)
• Sleep disturbances and sleeplessness
• Excessive tiredness
• Dermatological conditions such as acne, rosacea, psoriasis, and eczema
• Excessive sleeping
• Bruxism (and other dental complications)
• Memory problems
• Sexual dysfunction
• Perpetually vigilant (to the point of overwhelming fatigue)
• Substance misuse: stimulants like caffeine, narcotics, consumption of excessive food, alcohol abuse, improper use of prescription medications, etc.
• Diminished immune response: frequently experiencing episodes of colds, flu, and infections
• Experiencing weight gain or weight loss
• Social anxiety
• A sense of melancholy and diminished emotional state

The profound impact of stress and anxiety on both the physical and mental aspects of an individual is truly astounding. This list possesses an extensive range of items, the enumeration of which could feasibly occupy the entirety of this book (although I shall refrain from doing so).

In view of stress's profound influence on our physiological well-being, it is imperative for us to acquire a precise comprehension of the intricate processes that occur within our bodies during encounters with external stressors or internal psychological difficulties. In the subsequent chapter, we will undertake this very task and delve into the physiological mechanisms that assist our body in combating the overwhelming situation, albeit at the expense of our well-being and contentment.

Step 2: Addressing Anxiety during the Incipient Stage

Having identified the factors that induce your anxiety and its underlying cause, your subsequent course of action entails addressing the onset of anxiousness when triggered. Anxiety exhibits a series of distinct stages, and the longer it persists and progresses to subsequent stages, the greater the likelihood of experiencing a complete manifestation of an anxiety attack. One might inquire about the strategies employed in managing anxiety during the initial onset. There are two approaches that may be employed for managing anxiety during its initial stage of activation: trigger prevention and trigger desensitization.

Trigger Prevention Method

This concerns the identification of a method to mitigate the onset of the stimulus which precipitates the anxiety episode. As an illustration, in the case where you are experiencing apprehension regarding a forthcoming event that can be canceled, the approach based on trigger prevention would recommend the cancellation of said event. Similarly, if you frequently suffer from anxiety attacks while traveling by air, opting to cancel your flight could potentially alleviate your anxiety symptoms. In the event of trigger prevention, you will be required to forego air travel and instead opt for ground transportation. `

While this method may be functional, it is not optimal as it appears to be more akin to evading the issue. Furthermore, there exist circumstances beyond your jurisdiction which are irrefutable and cannot be preempted or revoked. As an example, consider a mandatory proficiency examination essential for securing a job advancement.

By employing this approach, one is essentially not actively addressing anxiety, but rather allowing it to intensify each time the trigger is avoided. If one desires to combat and conquer anxiety, the subsequent approach proves to be the most effective and suitable in this endeavor.

Trigger Desensitization Method

To facilitate your comprehension of this approach, it is imperative that I elucidate the concept of sensitization. Sensitization refers to the process through which one's mind or body is conditioned to respond to specific psychological or physical stimuli in an exaggerated or unfavorable manner.

This programming is consistently not done with conscious intent; it is plausible to inadvertently program one's mind to develop heightened sensitivity towards a given stimulus. For instance, if one experiences strong aversion towards clowns or any other object, it is imperative to acknowledge the origins of this sentiment as being non-innate or inherent in human nature. Instead, you unwittingly conditioned yourself during your initial exposure to the object or occurrence to elicit a negative response. Nonetheless, it is noteworthy that one possesses the ability to reprogram oneself through the implementation of the desensitization technique, thereby mitigating the extent of sensitivity.

Dr. Claire Weekers introduced a highly effective method for acknowledging and diminishing fear through the implementation of the 'Recognize 2nd Fear' exercise. This exercise pertains to promptly detecting and effectively suppressing any initial or subtle manifestations of anxiety. The commencement of the anxiety may manifest as either the exclamation "Oh My Gosh" or the declaration "I am going to perish." The most effective course of action in that particular instance would be to exercise control over your imagination. For example, in the event that you perceive a threat to your own mortality, it would be advisable to pause and engage in a thorough analysis of the underlying reasons supporting this perception.

The further you engage in a thorough analysis of your imagination and the given circumstances, the more evident it becomes that your response to a situation lacks justification. This realization empowers you to gradually perceive the anxiety as groundless.

Third Step: Manage and Prevail over the Onset of Anxiety

In the event that you were unable to effectively manage the anxiety during the initial trigger phase, how might you address a subsequent instance of a severe anxiety attack? What strategies can be employed to combat anxiety in individuals who are already affected by it? As previously stated, anxiety attacks progress through various phases and intensify if left unaddressed for an extended period of time. "In circumstances where one is not adequately equipped to address the issue during its initial onset, it remains possible to surmount the episode of anxiety by implementing the subsequent measures:

Incorporate Deep Breathing Techniques: When confronted with feelings of anxiety or experiencing an anxiety episode, the initial step is to incorporate deep breathing techniques. In the majority of instances, individuals experiencing an anxiety attack tend to engage in rapid, shallow breathing which results in insufficient oxygen intake. Unfortunately, this exacerbates the situation. Proper engagement in deep respiration is of utmost importance, as it guarantees the adequate intake of oxygen and allows for introspection and contemplation regarding one's emotions. Could you please elucidate your method of engaging in deep breathing exercises?

Please position your right hand on your chest area, while resting your left hand gently upon your abdominal region. Inhale deeply through your nasal passages and proceed to exhale through your oral cavity. While engaging in rhythmic breathing, commence a countdown from the number 10 to 1. Should you fail to achieve a state of tranquility following the aforementioned breathing exercise, it is permissible to repeat it until a tangible sense of calmness permeates your nervous system. On certain occasions, it may be necessary to perform up to 10 repetitions in order to alleviate your nervousness, contingent upon the severity of the anxiety episode.

Engage in Contemplation: Given that anxiety attacks often stem from pessimistic anticipation of a potential event, consider dedicating a brief moment to envisioning a more positive outcome for said event. As an example, if the anxiety attack arises from your apprehension about an upcoming medical appointment, you can allocate a few moments to mentally envision the desired outcome you wish to achieve during your visit. One may envision a scenario where the doctor's appointment yields a positive outcome and actually brings about a pleasant experience. The greater extent to which you engage in visualization, the more your subconscious mind perceives it as factual, as it lacks the ability to distinguish between reality and imagination. Consequently, it is probable that you will experience a marginally more convenient experience during your visit to the doctor.

Promptly Execute Measures: Directly following the visualization process, endeavor to undertake proactive measures towards materializing your desired outcome. This represents the ultimate measure to prevail over an imminent episode of anxiety. Expeditiously implementing measures will reveal the true nature of your apprehension, namely, a transient sentiment. Returning to the previous illustration, the subsequent course of action entails availing oneself of the subsequent bus or train in order to reach one's doctor's office punctually for the scheduled appointment. It is advisable not to engage in avoidance behaviors towards tasks that provoke anxiety, as such tendencies tend to perpetuate and exacerbate the anxious feelings over time. Therefore, it is imperative to confront anxiety directly.

Negative Emotions

Negative emotions are inherent in the human experience; nevertheless, individuals allocate the majority of their time evading the task of managing these adverse sentiments. Negative emotions are perceived as the sentiments that elicit profound distress and intense sorrow in an individual. Adverse emotions have the potential to induce aversion towards oneself or others, consequently diminishing one's self-esteem and self-assurance.

Certain emotions that frequently undergo a transformation into negative states include anger, resentment, sorrow, and envy. Nevertheless, within an appropriate context, such sentiments are inherently and entirely normal. When negative emotions manifest at inopportune moments or in an inappropriate manner, an individual's zest for life may wane. The most effective means of circumventing this occurrence involves an individual exercising restraint in allowing their adverse emotions to excessively impact their emotional state, and consciously opting against exhibiting their negative sentiments in an unfavorable manner.

It is imperative that individuals acquire knowledge and consistently bear in mind that prolonged harboring of negative emotions can lead to a gradual descent into a negative pattern of behaviors and thoughts. In the midst of a period of decline, adverse emotions will impede an individual's capacity for logical thinking and rational behavior. This will consequently result in an individual's inability to perceive situations in the most objective manner, as their preoccupation with viewing situations through a lens of personal bias and selectively recalling memories will hinder their ability to accurately assess reality. Therefore, the adverse sentiment, such as indignation or sorrow, serves to hinder individuals from deriving satisfaction in their existence.

The more protracted the occurrence of a descending whirlwind, the more entrenched the predicament ultimately becomes. The identical problem may arise if an individual resorts to addressing their adverse emotions through improper or detrimental means. As an illustration, in the event that an individual opts to manifest their anger by means of physical aggression, it not only constitutes an unsuitable course of action, but also poses harm to all parties implicated.

Additionally, it is imperative to consider the comprehensive intricacy of emotional responses when examining negative emotions. The experience of emotions encompasses both psychological and physiological aspects, as emotions are influenced by both cognitive processes and sensory perceptions. This implies that the cognitive processes in individuals trigger the release of specific chemicals and hormones in the brain, subsequently inducing a heightened state of arousal. Every emotional response occurs in this manner, regardless of whether it is negative or positive in nature.

The procedure involved is intricate, and individuals often lack the appropriate aptitude to effectively manage their adverse sentiments. This constitutes the primary factor contributing to individuals' struggle in effectively managing their encounters related to adverse emotional states.

An effective strategy to facilitate an individual's acquisition of improved emotional management skills entails the process of categorizing their negative emotions. The five primary categories of negative emotions commence with sadness, which is correlated with depression, despondency, and desolation. The subsequent classification pertains to anxiety, wherein it is intricately linked to episodes of panic, anguish, apprehension, uneasiness, and trepidation. The subsequent classification pertains to anger, which is inherently associated with sentiments of annoyance, irritation, frustration, and rage. The final two categories consist of guilt and embarrassment.

Once an individual becomes cognizant of the specific negative emotion they are experiencing, they must subsequently examine the underlying automatic thoughts that are giving rise to said emotion. Once this task has been completed as well, individuals will gain the capacity to truly grasp the emotions they experience within the context of any given category among the five.

The notions that are commonly linked with the classification of sadness encompass introspective thoughts, thoughts of inadequacy or deficiency, and gloomy thoughts. The primary cognitions associated with the anxiety category encompass thoughts pertaining to threats, risks, or perils, speculative thoughts encapsulating potential scenarios, and thoughts regarding the occurrence of something horrific in the future.

The anger category primarily pertains to thoughts concerning potential harm or perceived injustice, cognitive processes involving obligations or expectations, and contemplations on the violation of established regulations. The emotions linked to the guilt category encompass contemplation of actions that contradict one's moral compass, consideration of one's accountability for potential adverse consequences, and notions pertaining to causing harm to others. Finally, the embarrassment category encompasses reflections on the potential scrutiny and evaluation by others due to one's imperfections or errors.

In most cases, when an individual undergoes a negative emotional state, that emotion can be categorized within one of the five aforementioned classifications. Additionally, there exist instances in which a sensation may be applicable to multiple classifications concurrently.

Frenemies Of Anxiety

There are no definitive etiological factors associated with anxiety disorders that have been empirically substantiated. As per the findings from the National Institute of Mental Health, a substantial body of research has supported the notion that an amalgamation of environmental and genetic influences significantly contributes to the onset of anxiety. The examination of brain chemistry has additionally been scrutinized as a plausible factor, as specific regions of the brain that govern fear responses may be implicated.

The vast majority of anxiety disorders arise concomitantly with various health conditions, encompassing mental disorders like depression and disorders associated with substance misuse. The majority of individuals afflicted with anxiety attempt to alleviate the symptoms of panic attacks through the consumption of alcoholic beverages or the use of illicit substances, exacerbating their condition further. The transient nature of solace offered by alcohol and drugs is evident. Studies have revealed that the consumption of nicotine, alcohol, illicit substances, and even caffeine can exacerbate any form of anxiety disorder.

While further research is warranted, it is asserted by experts that anxiety disorders encompass a confluence of various elements, encompassing genetics, stress, and dietary factors.

The scientific literature on twins indicates that genetic factors can exert significant influence. A research article published in the journal PloS ONE proposed a potential association between the RBFOX1 gene and the emergence of anxiety disorders, including generalized anxiety disorder, by influencing their pathogenesis and progression. The research demonstrated that there is an equal contribution from both non-genetic and genetic factors.

Additional areas of the brain, such as the hippocampus and amygdala, are also currently under investigation. The amygdala is a small, almond-shaped organ situated in the depths of the brain, responsible for the regulation of emotions and the analysis of potential dangers. Each instance of perceiving signs of threat or danger results in the transmission of a signal from your amygdala to the remainder of your brain.

Researchers propose that it has the potential to elicit an anxiety-inducing reaction and precipitate episodes of panic. The amygdala has a significant impact on anxiety disorders characterized by specific phobias, such as phobias of insects, flying, water-related situations, or enclosed spaces.

Conversely, your hippocampus can potentially elevate your vulnerability to developing specific anxiety disorders. The cerebral region tasked with the storage of memories, encompassing those pertaining to potentially perilous or menacing occurrences. According to experts, individuals with a history of military service or childhood abuse are believed to exhibit a relatively diminished size of the hippocampus.

"There are additional factors that can elevate your susceptibility to anxiety:

In relation to gender, the prevalence of generalized anxiety disorder and other anxiety conditions is twofold higher among females compared to males.

Experiencing severe trauma, such as military combat or instances of child abuse, can elevate the likelihood of developing anxiety. This encompass factors such as being an observer of a distressing event, residing in close proximity to an individual who has experienced trauma, or personally enduring traumatic experiences.

Personality classification: Individuals with specific personality traits are more susceptible to developing anxiety disorders. Individuals who are highly strung and possess type A personalities are particularly susceptible to this potential risk.

In the realm of genetics, if a member of your immediate family has experienced or is currently experiencing an anxiety disorder, it increases the likelihood of you developing a similar condition. Children whose parents suffer from anxiety disorders are at an elevated risk.

Stress: It is an inevitable aspect of our daily lives that we must all confront. Stress can be seen as a potentially beneficial factor, as it possesses the ability to drive individuals towards progress and aid in surmounting challenges. Nevertheless, unaddressed, excessive, or persistent stress can elevate the likelihood of developing a long-term manifestation of anxiety.

Medical intervention: Every medical intervention is accompanied by potential cognitive and physiological repercussions. Some medications have the potential to elicit restlessness, fluctuations in mood, and a sense of exhaustion, all of which can contribute to feelings of anxiety.

Furthermore, the likelihood of developing an anxiety disorder is increased when there is a coexistence of other anxiety disorders, a prior record of substance abuse, irritable bowel syndrome, and depression.

As previously stated, the precise etiology of anxiety disorders remains elusive, yet there exist factors that significantly contribute to their development. One's personal background, surrounding circumstances, and genetic makeup significantly contribute in this aspect.

Certain medications and medical conditions may give rise to symptoms reminiscent of anxiety disorders. Therefore, it is imperative to seek guidance from a qualified expert who can assess your potential susceptibility to anxiety or ascertain its specific classification.

PART TWO

Initiating Conversations: Engagement Through Casual Discussion

Key Information Regarding Casual Conversations

The concept of "Small Talk" is not as ancient as the human civilization, should you have entertained such a thought.

Casual conversation serves as a means for individuals to establish professional relationships, facilitating an avenue for discussing potential opportunities. When seeking to establish professional connections, engaging in casual conversation fosters a sense of relaxation, encourages active involvement, and establishes a conducive atmosphere for relationship-building.

Is It Really Important?

In my opinion, it is not the case.

Nevertheless, the current societal standards dictate that it is an essential characteristic and quality of an accomplished individual. It is revered within the realm of emerging entrepreneurs, as well as among the socially engaged elite, as an essential possession. This phenomenon is particularly prevalent within the Self-Help industry, as evidenced by the abundance of uplifting seminars and numerous books being marketed.

What constitutes as small talk?

I regard any conversation that deviates from

> Improves me,

> Entertains me,

> Facilitates my growth and development, > Supports my personal and professional advancement, > Contributes to my overall progress and

improvement, > Encourages my learning and skill-building.

to be considered as informal conversation.

Nevertheless, this depiction proves to be excessively challenging for the global population. I am of the opinion that there exists an appropriate context and moment for engaging in "Small Talk" within the confines of a business meeting. This serves as a means to gradually transition into more meaningful discussions, such as when acquainting oneself with others for the first time. However, individuals whom you are already acquainted with and encounter on a regular, if not daily, basis do not require it. The warm-up can simply consist of a simple greeting to initiate a genuine conversation. Why would that be? In my personal viewpoint, the inquiry that seems devoid of purpose in the realm of "Small Talk" is, in my estimation, the commonly asked question of "How are you?". It appears that individuals do not genuinely seek information pertaining to your emotional state; rather, they anticipate the anticipated response of "I'm fine, how about yourself?", merely enabling them to offer their pre-programmed reply.

Furthermore, there exists another individual of noteworthy conversational abilities, commonly referred to as the 'Small Talkers' hero, who possesses an extraordinary aptitude for engaging in captivating discussions pertaining to environmental matters or recounting recent events from another person's life, all within a brief window of a few minutes. I am completely unaware of the details regarding the how and why of this situation. These individuals have the potential to erode your cognitive faculties and disrupt your inner tranquility within the confines of an elevator or when engaged in conversation pertaining to subject matters which hold little personal relevance to you, but are of great import to them.

Strategies for Engaging in Casual Conversations

There are four strategies that will assist you in engaging in casual conversation in any given circumstance.

First, ask open-ended questions. Numerous individuals possess a tendency to engage in self-discussion, as we inherently find ourselves the most intriguing subjects. Moreover, it proves more advantageous to converse about oneself than to engage in discourse concerning individuals about whom we possess limited or no knowledge. Consider this: Which would present a greater challenge for you - acquiring knowledge about the art of glass-blowing during the 14th century, or delving into the depths of your treasured book? Open-ended inquiries foster an invigorating and vibrant dialogue, prompting the interlocutor to express themselves more openly.

Second, practice active listening. Occasionally, it may be tempting to disengage, but by diligently focusing, you will cultivate significantly more robust connections. The other individual will note how you seem focused. Furthermore, if one does not listen with divided attention, they can more effortlessly inquire about pertinent matters and retain information for future reference.

Furthermore, please kindly refrain from using your mobile device. When we experience discomfort or a lack of confidence in social settings, we often resort to our phones, which can greatly hinder our ability to effectively communicate and connect with others. There is a limited likelihood of individuals approaching you if you are engrossed in your cellphone screen, and it conveys a clear indication to those with whom you are already engaged in conversation that you lack interest.

Fourth, show your enthusiasm. Engaging in casual conversation does not necessarily foster a depression-free environment. Nevertheless, if you approach it with the appropriate mindset, you can derive enjoyment from it. Regard these discussions as opportunities for others to deepen their understanding. You can never anticipate the individuals you may encounter or the insights they may offer - thus, seize the opportunity for a remarkable exchange of ideas.

Possessing exceptional conversational skills will not only facilitate engaging discussions, but also mitigate apprehension when navigating uncharted environments.

1. The location

Discuss your surroundings. Are you located in a pleasant residential setting, a domestic environment, or a commercial district? Is the town noteworthy? Have you recently had the opportunity to visit any interesting nearby locales?

2. Entertainment

Discuss what you have consistently felt a sense of longing for and what has recently captured your attention. This could encompass any of your activities such as indulging in a Netflix series, the most recent film you watched, the books you are assessing, the performances you are attending, and similar endeavors.

3. Art

If the individual whom you are conversing with holds a deep appreciation for art, inquire about the museums they have previously visited and would consider visiting again. Additionally, prompt them to share their admiration for particular artists, any critiques they may have written regarding galleries, their most cherished exhibitions, preferred forms of art and media, and the manner in which their passion for the arts developed.

You also have the capability to assess transformations within the realm of art. Is there any particular area of current interest for them in the realm of creative pursuits, akin to the exploration of 'post-internet art'? What is your opinion regarding them?

4. Food

Cuisine is a highly effective topic for casual conversation, as the majority of individuals possess a fondness for culinary pursuits. Kindly assess the recommended restaurants and dishes, determining your own preferences. Kindly inquire about their preferred dishes for home cooking, considering their infrequent outings to dine. Outline a prospective situation and elicit their perspective on the preferred choice of cuisine or contribution to the occasion. If a total of ten individuals are attending the gathering, this includes two individuals adhering to a vegan diet, one individual with a nut allergy, and an additional individual abstaining from consuming gluten. May I seek your recommendation?

5. Interests and leisure activities

Explore the interests and passions of the individual in question. They will undoubtedly experience enthusiasm when contemplating their personal interests, providing you with an opportunity to establish a deeper connection with them.

Inquire about their leisure activities, their involvement in extracurricular pursuits beyond the workplace, their evolving interests from childhood to the present, any educational or instructional endeavors they are engaged in, and their aspirations in various domains such as sushi-making, short story-writing, salsa dancing, and the like.

6. Work

Discussing your professional occupations can be challenging. It is important to avoid the conversation turning into a mundane exchange of professions, as it tends to happen unless redirected towards more captivating subjects.

Conversely, work serves as an excellent conversation topic, given that most individuals possess an abundance of experiences and insights to share.

Instead of inquiring about common topics such as your current employment, its duration, and your fondness towards it, consider engaging with compelling and unforeseen queries such as:

My [niece/son/grandchild] harbors aspirations to pursue a career in [profession]. Do you have any concepts or suggestions that I can relay?

What particular facet of your job do you favor? What factors influenced your decision to pursue employment at Walmart?

What are the skills you are leveraging the most in your professional endeavors? Is that in accordance with your anticipated outcome?

What are commonly held perceptions or generalizations associated with the profession of [job title]? Does it withstand scrutiny?

Did you fail to anticipate any aspects of that role? What are your thoughts on it?"

7. Sports

Certain individuals have the propensity to engage in continuous discussions pertaining to sports. Others prefer to engage in conversations about any topic except for that one. There exist several guiding principles for engaging in conversations pertaining to sports.

Initially, in the event that you find yourself among a collective of two or more individuals, it is important to ensure that each individual possesses an interest in sports. You should avoid the act of excluding an individual's participation.

Furthermore, engaging in an enthusiastic conversation may be enjoyable; however, participating in a contentious discussion will not in any way contribute to the achievement of your networking objectives. If either party becomes agitated, it is advisable to redirect the conversation to a different subject.

8. The Weather

Discussing the weather holds universal appeal as a common topic in casual conversation. It\'s typically not the most scintillating conversation-starter, but with a little creativity, you can spark some engaging discussions.

Inquire about the intended activities of the individual in consideration of the prevailing weather conditions, such as whether they intend to remain indoors and engage in cinematic pursuits on a rainy day. If the weather is favorable, do they plan to engage in outdoor activities such as having a barbecue, participating in outdoor recreation, going on a hike, or dining al fresco on their patio?

Furthermore, a topic of conversation can be their preferred climate and the underlying reasons for their preferences. This often evolves into a discourse on their character traits, which can be enjoyable and invigorating.

Initiate a conversation about the weather conditions prevalent in their place of origin. Does it diverge from the location at which they currently reside? The same? Which type do they derive greater enjoyment from? If individuals were given the option to select a place of residence solely based on climatic conditions, where would they prefer to dwell?

Seasonal rituals and traditions can also serve as convenient topics of conversation. Do they engage in any particular activities or customs during this time of year? Do they frequently go to any locations, engage in trips, meet with individuals, or partake in other forms of activities?

9. Travel

It is true that not all individuals whom you engage in conversation with will possess extensive travel experiences. However, inquiring about their recent encounters with intriguing destinations can lead to a plethora of opportunities for dialogue and exploration. Whether it involves brief excursions within an hour's radius, grand summer sojourns, or ambitious expeditions that fulfill personal aspirations, the query at hand possesses the ability to prompt even the most reticent individuals to divulge impassioned recollections or eagerly anticipate forthcoming escapades.

Ensure that you possess a set of additional inquiries regarding their intended activities during their journey. What cuisines they are most enthusiastic about sampling. And the anticipated mementos they intend to procure for their return.

10. Their Local Favorites

HubSpot's Director of Sales, Dan Tyre, provides a valuable technique accessible to all representatives. Prior to a scheduled conversation with a potential client, he conducts online research on the town/city where they reside by utilizing the search engine platform, Google. Frequently, the individuals with whom he is having conversations reside in cities that Dan has never personally experienced. However, through a brief two-minute inquiry, he becomes informed about their most popular newly established dining establishment, the current local weather conditions, and the preferred landmarks revered by residents.

He applies his understanding to impress potential clients with inquiries such as, "Have you had the opportunity to experience [Insert recent prominent local theater production]?" or "Are you managing to keep comfortable in your current location?" I have heard that temperatures are expected to reach the 90s this week. By taking this additional step, it creates a sense of comfort for the potential client, indicating Dan's genuine interest in their concerns and establishes an instant connection.

6: The Interview Process

Various Interview Formats

During the job application process, individuals may encounter various types of interviews. The process typically commences with initial correspondence either via email or by telephone communication. Usually, the human resources department or the company's manager will reach out to you for the purpose of scheduling an interview and determining a mutually convenient time. The HR department will select a time slot that is convenient for them and subsequently provide you with a selection of interview time options. It all commences with something akin to this: " "It all initiates with something resembling this: " "It all starts with something of this nature: " "It all originates with something along these lines: " "It all originates from something similar to this:

Dear applicant,

After careful examination of your credentials and qualifications, we have determined that you are an exceptionally qualified candidate. We kindly request to move forward with the evaluation of your application. Would you have any availability for a telephone interview on Friday between the hours of 1pm and 3pm? Please inform us of your preferred timing. We eagerly anticipate receiving your response.

Best regards,

Human Resources Department of X____
"

The initial stage of the procedure entails conducting a telephonic interview.

The initial stage of the procedure can manifest in various ways, nonetheless it may commence with the assessment of application documents. Upon discerning that your application captures the interest of the HR team, they will consequently advance to the subsequent phase, typically involving an informal interview, such as a telephonic interview. This can present a significant challenge for individuals, as the inability to visually interact with others can lead to a disconcerting and exasperating experience of impersonal communication. Nevertheless, there exist certain guidelines that must be adhered to during a telephone interview, which shall be delineated subsequently.

1. Please provide a succinct overview of your background and articulate your motivations for seeking employment with our organization.

2. Please refrain from remaining silent during our telephone conversation. During the course of the interview, it is advisable to employ non-verbal cues, such as affirmative murmurs or other similar gestures, to effectively demonstrate your attentiveness to the interviewer. They would prefer not to entertain the notion that you have become unaccounted for, either in the bathroom or elsewhere.

3. Strive for conciseness and clarity during your interview. Please refrain from divulging excessive amounts of information at this preliminary phase. Inquire about several matters during the interview.

4. Express gratitude to the interviewer for their valuable time and consideration in conducting the interview with you. It is imperative to consistently demonstrate gratitude when extended an invitation to an interview.

5. Do not hesitate to leave a lasting impression during this phase. It is

imperative to convey an air of attentiveness and enthusiasm regarding the position, although the true dedication and effort commences subsequent to the phone interview.

The telephonic interview generally serves as an informative interview, enabling the identification and elimination of candidates who lack genuine interest in the position. Assuming you have demonstrated sincere interest in the position, it is probable that the employer will be inclined to advance your application further. However, it is crucial that you indicate to the company that you have conducted a preliminary evaluation of both their organization and the requirements of the job. Ensuring that you have diligently examined the job description and announcement is imperative to being prepared to address all facets discussed during this informational interview.

Following the telephonic interview, the application process may unfold in either of two possible directions. It may proceed to a Skype interview, or it may progress to an in-person interview. Frequently, the Skype interview will precede the in-person interview.

Virtual video conference interview

This interview presents a nuanced challenge as one must strike a delicate balance between appearing relaxed and confident while maintaining a professional demeanor and avoiding excessive informality. When attending an interview with a company, it is crucial to dress professionally as it will demonstrate your commitment and suitability for the position. If you are conducting the interview within the confines of your residence, it is advisable to minimize the presence of any potential disruptions in the background. The most suitable setting for your interview would ideally entail a simple white backdrop, though occasionally, this may not be feasible. Nevertheless, provided that your apartment or dwelling is maintained in a neat and organized manner, the presence of an alternative backdrop should not pose any issues.

Furthermore, aside from ensuring the appropriateness of your background and the suitability of your interview venue, it is imperative to verify the functionality of your camera as well as the optimal performance of the audio. This is of utmost importance, as it is imperative to avoid any occurrence of technical difficulties during the interview, despite the potential inevitability of such issues even when you are excessively prepared. It is highly advisable to make preparations well in advance in order to ensure timely commencement.

Ensure that your notes are easily accessible, but exercise caution in positioning them so as to not make them overtly visible to the interviewer. It is advisable to avoid giving the impression of reciting from a prepared script during the interview, as this could potentially create a negative impression and discourage the interviewer. It is imperative to ensure that your speech comes across in a natural manner. Therefore, it is advisable to have a few notes prepared to refer to in the event of temporary memory loss, but it is important to avoid fixating on a written script during the task.

It is imperative to direct your gaze towards the camera during a Skype interview, as this demonstrates a genuine and attentive engagement with the conversation, potentially enhancing your chances of securing a higher evaluation. A stronger on-camera presence increases the likelihood of progressing to subsequent rounds of interviews, especially those involving face-to-face interactions.

Prior to initiating the call, it is imperative to ascertain whether the employer intends to contact you and make suitable preparations accordingly. Preemptively ascertain the individual responsible for commencing the call and prepare yourself to promptly attend to the incoming call without delay.

After gaining access to the call, the interview process commences. It is imperative that you exhibit exemplary conduct throughout the duration of the call. Please refrain from engaging in excessive fidgeting or expressing exaggerated body language cues, and exercise moderation in facial expressions, ensuring not to smile excessively. Maintaining a composed and self-assured demeanor while refraining from excessive gesticulation or appearing overly confident is crucial during a Skype interview. Rather, it is advisable to remain composed and refrain from excessive screen usage. The capabilities of the Skype interface have inherent limitations, which necessitates one utilizing them to their advantage rather than suffering any detrimental consequences as a result. The extent of your presentation that the interviewer can perceive is limited. To begin with, their field of vision is limited to your upper torso. Nevertheless, it is imperative that you refrain from donning a suit jacket while simultaneously adorning shorts or boxers during the course of your conversation with the interviewer. It is imperative that you make adequate preparations for this interview, treating it with the same level of formality as any other professional interview. Henceforth, it is imperative for you to be attired appropriately and adequately prepared to perform exemplary throughout the procedure.

Please take note of the interview's timing. Provided that the duration of the process exceeds initial expectations, it can be inferred that you are being regarded as a highly promising candidate and that the interviewer holds a favorable view of you. On average, a Skype interview typically spans a duration of 20 to 40 minutes; however, in certain instances, it may extend to an hour. Generally, in the event that your interview is constrained by time, it is anticipated that the outcome will be unfavorable. If an interviewer develops a favorable impression of you, they will likely be inclined to allocate additional time for the evaluation of your application and thorough examination of your profile. They will exhibit authentic enthusiasm towards your candidacy, as they have a strong desire to employ you. Regard the extension of time required as an indication that your application is poised to receive commendable scores.

A subsequent interview with the Skype interviewer might be structured as follows:

"Esteemed interviewer,

We extend our gratitude for your valuable time and willingness to participate in the Skype interview with us. We were thoroughly impressed by the merits highlighted in your application and profile, and hereby express our intention to advance your application to the next stage. Would it be possible for you to participate in a face-to-face interview at our corporate headquarters on _____ at _____? We eagerly anticipate receiving your response. Have a great day.

Best regards,

Human Resources Department of _____

Face-to-face interview" or "In-person interview

Subsequent to the preliminary evaluation, the HR team will make a determination regarding extending an invitation for a face-to-face interview at the company's premises. The personal interview is regarded as a culmination of the process and necessitates extensive preparation, encompassing matters such as attire, communication, and additional considerations. The personal interview will serve as a platform on which you must demonstrate your depth of knowledge and suitability for the position in question. Hence, it is advisable to thoroughly prepare oneself for the interview.

Group interview

The panel interview is regarded as a highly demanding mode of assessment, as it entails direct competition with other candidates in a confined setting. One might perceive that you are compelled to outpace all individuals present in the vicinity. Group interviews are commonly conducted either before or after an initial individual interview in the context of corporate settings, as an integral component of the candidate selection process. Please find outlined herein several steps that can be adhered to in order to enhance one's success in navigating this process.

1. Conduct preliminary research on the interview venue and familiarize yourself with the company's background. Prioritize acquiring comprehensive knowledge about the company to impress the interviewers with your profound understanding of their organization.

2. Please make sure to arrive at the interview venue at least 25-30 minutes prior to the scheduled time in order to

familiarize yourself with the surroundings and engage in preparatory tasks.

3. Do not attempt to outpace or surpass the other candidates in terms of competition. Please demonstrate respect towards others and their responses, refraining from attempting to intimidate them or deter their participation when asked a question.

4. Please do not hesitate to respond. On occasion, it is incumbent upon oneself to be the initial respondent to inquiries. On separate occasions, it is possible for you to lend support to your fellow interviewees during their responses. Nevertheless, the utmost priority lies in exuding a self-assured demeanor devoid of excessive conceit or hubris.

5. Exhibit frequent smiles and nods throughout the interview as a demonstration of politeness and adherence to the customary social norms associated with the proceedings. In addition, endeavor to display utmost

kindness and graciousness towards every individual. Although it is accurate that there is competition among the other candidates, it is imperative that you display utmost regard and civility towards all individuals involved. It is not merely a cutthroat or ruthless perspective.

6. Express your gratitude to the interviewer as well as your fellow interviewees, and extend a gesture of farewell by shaking hands with them subsequent to the interview. Furthermore, it is essential to express your sincere appreciation and extend gratitude to all individuals involved in the interview process as it draws to a conclusion. This will exhibit an attitude of humbleness and delicacy, qualities that can significantly contribute to your success in securing the job.

Ultimately, these recommendations will greatly assist you throughout the interview process and in securing the coveted position that aligns with your aspirations. Every individual step holds significance, however, it is imperative that you possess a comprehensive understanding of the specific actions required during each interview in order to enhance your prospects of achieving success in the job application process.

www.ingramcontent.com/pod-product-compliance
Lightning Source LLC
Chambersburg PA
CBHW050247120526
44590CB00016B/2254